If I Write It, It Can Heal

IF I WRITE IT, IT CAN HEAL

Emily Claudette Freeman

All rights reserved. Printed in the United States of America.

No part of this book may be used or reproduced in any manner whatsoever, without written permission of the author or a legal representative; except in the case of quotations embodied in critical articles or reviews.

©February 2012, Emily Claudette Freeman
Edited by Tymira Mack

Published by Pecan Tree Publishing, Hollywood, Fl

www.pecantreebooks.com

Library of Congress: 2013901000

ISBN: 978-0-9888969-0-1

Other Titles by Emily (E.) Claudette Freeman:
Pieces. And Me. A Collection of Life
Sheltered Deliverance
The Morning Hour: Arise, Write, Release
Fabulous You Power Nuggets
When I Danced With God

PECAN TREE PUBLISHING
Hollywood, Fl.
www.pecantreepress.com

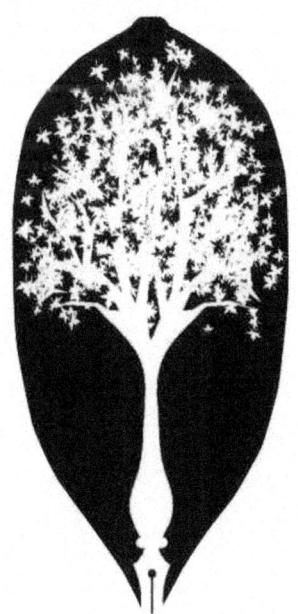

New Voices | New Styles | New Vision

Dedications

To my son, Isaiah Langston-Michael Freeman – I am honored, humbled and blessed to have a child that asks me every day, "Do you know how much I love you?" He has taught me to love through it all.

To my nephew, Douglas Tirrell Freeman, Jr. – I hope in these words you find the inner power for which you continue to search. You are a jewel and a child of the Most High God. It is all in Him, and therefore, it is absolutely all in you.

To my niece, Camisha Ann Freeman – you are a true diva; divine, innovative, vivacious and altogether lovely. Go take the world as only you can. Just remember – taking it – means taking risks that others may not support or applaud – still take the world and enjoy the journey.

To my other babies, LaRenna and Amir, RJ, my buddy Tamijah, Cailin, and Deion – I love you all to life!

To Prophetess Robin McCray, Vicki Antonio, Charlene Bouie, Min. E. Chantaye Watson, Yoruba Priestess Yeyefini Efundolade, Rev. Reckel Ferguson, Elder Brenda Jackson, Beverly Jackson, Min. Craig Stafford, Carol Watson, Dr. Deborah Jones-Allen, Tymira Mack and Elder Vikki Johnson – thank you for speaking into, prophesying into, pulling my power forward and allowing me to share it with others; and placing my words and God's Words back in my heart through tumultuous years of awakening. May God do more than you can ever imagine in each of your lives.

*For every woman and man that reads these words
and feels the pain, release, awareness and
truth that life can bring – if you write it,
you can begin to heal and walk through the lesson
of each and every experience.*

Table of Contents

The Writing is on the Wall 1

Life on Purpose 5

My Foolishness Said Give Up 9

Oh You are Just Too Excited 14

I May not be a Fist-to-Fist Fighter, But I Sure Think Like One 18

I am not a Cigarette, So Please Don't Drag on Me 23

Affirm Your Life 28

God Tones are - Well - Not to be Ignored 32

Child, I Got Me a Gift 36

The Man the Good Samaritan Helped 40

Listen - Before you Need a Recovery Plan 44

I Have a Love Jones for Me 49

Go Ahead, Get on the Plane 53

Dreamer get on Board – The Plane is Here 60

My Design, My Style, My Me 69

The Inauguration of a Dreamer 73

A Will for the Demons in your Life 77

Why is there a Coffin Under There 81

I Could have been more Disobedient but I am
So Glad God Kicked me into Obedience Instead 85

The Oil - Overfilled 90

Talk to the Hand 95

Turning on my Power 99

The Couch's Bedtime Tale 104

Why Now? 108

About the Author 113

*If I Write It,
It Can Heal*

The Writing is on the Wall

Have you ever experienced this? It is the middle of a horrible week and you feel totally overwhelmed. If one more thing gets added to your schedule, YOU WILL ABSOLUTELY GO CRAZY! On the other hand, perhaps your frustration sounds more like this, "Oh God - there cannot be another problem centered on me - can there?" Here is a truth we must realize as life begins to feel unbearable: We must clear the proverbial and literal clutter from every fiber of our being. Clutter chokes even the simplest thoughts. In these times, we really just want to find a quiet spot and awaken it with our screams. When we find ourselves in the place of too much clutter; and not enough clarity to get through it, we have to do one pivotal thing – STOP! Stop thinking. Stop processing. Stop accessing. Stop assuming. Stop the what-if scenarios. JUST STOP!

Look at the writing on the wall. Seriously, take a big sheet of paper, like a large Post-it pad; or a paper bag ripped open or a piece of construction paper and apply it to a wall, if you want, fill one whole wall with paper. Now listen; do not get caught up in what kind of paper! I say that because when we are inundated with problems, perplexities and negative possibilities, we begin to fixate on all the things that cannot help us focus on pushing through the darkness. So, do not allow the paper to become a continuing invitation to remain in a dark place. Once the paper is taped to the wall, your next step is to write words - BIG WORDS, little words, vertical words, affirming words and if you just need to - write profane words. The mission is to write. Write words that say what you feel. Write words that say what you want to feel. Write words that describe what you felt like when whatever happened

- happened. Write words that say what God is speaking to you - even as you write all over the wall.

Now, breathe. You've released it. Pull out your journal or start a journal, (again don't get caught up in the paper or journaling method) and have a talk with yourself about each word on the wall and watch the clutter slowly begin to organize. Watch how the clutter reveals how small and unnecessary some of the things invading you really are. You will begin to breathe easier as clutter, strife and stress leave your psyche. Once you do this something happens; peace fills the spot where an overwhelming feeling had become comfortable. Peace clears the way for fruitful and productive thought streams. Your mind and your spirit become centered again, and now the words on the wall change.

Be mindful of what I learned the hard way - you can only take care of the things that you can; the other things are in the hands of the divine God. When God feels you are ready to deal with those things - He will give you the wisdom to do so. I make it sound really easy, don't I? I assure you it is not. I have been through emotionally wrenching, professionally insulting and spiritually tumultuous times that have left me physically drained and of ill countenance. These were times that were eradicated or eased only through prayer and through my ability to write my truth without intimidation. My big words on the wall surely were similar to yours: STUPID, DESPERATE, WHAT WERE YOU THINKING, DAMN FOOL, and GOD DO YOU EVEN CARE. I know that our pain is never easy but it is a challenge of life that can be defeated and used as an awesome stepping stone to our ultimate life, spirit and soul success. Do not fret about tomorrow, baby it will bring its own stuff, I want you to remember this powerful truth that I am learning to be ALL TOO REAL - Sufficient is the grace you have for today.

... take a big sheet of paper, like a large Post-it pad; or a paper bag ripped open or a piece of construction paper and apply it to a wall, if you want, fill one whole wall with paper. Once the paper is taped to the wall, your next step is to write words - BIG WORDS, little words, vertical words, affirming words and if you just need to - write profane words. The mission is to write. Write words that say what you feel. Write words that say what you want to feel. Write words that describe what you felt like when whatever happened - happened. Write words that say what God is speaking to you - even as you write all over the wall:

Today write your future

Life on Purpose

One of the things I love about having an intimate relationship with God is the way He talks to us. I remember a particular season in my life that God began to consistently impart a very direct message about life on purpose and/or living on purpose. It came to me in at least three very clear and distinct ways during a week's span: in a book a friend suggested, in a Saturday morning meeting and in a worship service.

After those "pay attention" alerts, it was during a time of morning prayer and meditation that I had to face the fact that I simply gave up on so much of my living on purpose and living according to the things that really make me happy. I started to think about some of the goals that I wrote in my high school memory book and how I would envision my home adorned with art pieces vibrant with colors that speak to who I am. Somewhere along the way, I gave up on seeking out the things in people that wonderfully and positively challenged me, and I started to allow too many "just anybodies" into my life. While I have also learned to detox people, behaviors and insecurities, I was amazed in those quiet moments that morning about the amount of intrinsic joy and energy I had lost along the way.

I had to admit to myself, that I am still the woman who wants to have four sons frolicking around her, as I read books on a private beach. I am still the woman who wants to pick up and travel to wherever my imagination can take me on a whim. I am still the woman who envisions a house with a wrap-around porch and Southern summertime gatherings of artists, intellectuals and street corner philosophers, all sipping delightful elixirs as we mingle; and the kids taking over the yard. I am still the woman who wants to be surrounded and poured into by women of powerful integrity who can get super deep yet be more real than ever necessary. I see these women and me, at each gathering, pouring into another woman who needs that assurance and compassion. That is life on purpose for me.

So I decided on that day before my head hit the pillow for slumber and my son bear hugged me into a thirty minute conversation designed to prolong his bed time, that I was going to do something major to start my life on purpose anew. I decided to re-script my life completely and purposely according to those things that God implanted in me when He initially thought of me. As I re-write that script, I am doing so from a mindset that God can and will redeem not only the time, but also the energy lost to pursuing those things and people who were not part of my purpose. God can also restore those things designed for me that left me or that I pushed away. Honestly, I cannot really put a finger on when those divinely purposed matters left, how they left or why they did - but they have often resurfaced in my spirit and brought tears to my eyes as though they were mourning for me. Isn't that something? Your true spirit will mourn losing you when all it wants to do is live on purpose through you.

What does your life on purpose look like? Today, do not scribble something quickly in your journal, but really think about what your purposed life designed by The Spirit and the things of your spirit really look like? Write your way back to it. This is not about goals or to dos, no, this is about waking up every day and deciding that you have a purpose and every bit of your character, your decisions, your thoughts and your focus on that purpose should bring you joy. I am excited about having life on purpose - I pray you are as well.

What does your life on purpose look like? Today, do not scribble something quickly in your journal, but really think about what your purposed life designed by The Spirit and the things of your spirit really look like? Write your way back to it. This is not about goals or to dos, no, this is about waking up every day and deciding that you have a purpose:

Today write your future

My Foolishness Said Give Up

I am just going to admit it. There are some times, (a lot of times) I just want to give up. I just have to admit upfront that I have messed up royally (and repeatedly). I also have to admit and realize that I cannot fix much of the mess that I have created. I have felt like the rope of help being thrown down to me in my hole is still six feet too short. Have you ever felt that way? There are times, a lot of times I just want to give up. There are often people around me who encourage me to give up. I tell myself it would be so much easier to just throw in the towel. I may have one of those times tomorrow. I may have one of those times next year. Okay, on the real, I had one of those times yesterday. Then, after those two to five seconds (minutes) of pity, I got excited about my vision again; and I know that when those ho-hum moments resurface I will defeat them in that same excitement.

In what a lot of people have called absolutely crazy and not faith, in late summer 2007, I stepped away from a position as Station Manager of a gospel station to move into writing. The truth of the matter is, more than faith, God had begun to show me clearly that I was out of place there and while I could not communicate much of what I was feeling nor what had been spiritually revealed to anyone, I knew I had to go. So, in one of he hardest and most emotionally-drenching decisions I have ever made, I did just that – resigned. Fast forward three years and there I was a business owner who had to be brutally honest with herself. I said, with tears pouring and my nose red from the pressure of tears, "GIRL YOU HAVE MADE SOME HUGE BLUNDERS AND MISTAKES!" Some of my blunders led me back to my former boss to ask for financial help. I considered going back into the workforce. I felt my heart break over and over, each time I had to tell my son we could not afford something; especially when the something was a need and not a want. Yet, in all of that, I never lost sight of my vision. That vision is something I have talked about before - BIRTH.

When I began my solo writing career, it was about me. I was going to stage my own theatrical works and get them produced by others, while writing this list of books in my head. Ladada Ladadee. Ladadada. That was what I was going to do. Then suddenly I had this business of coaching people through their writing process. BIRTH. Then I found myself with this small publishing company that now has this grand vision and authors waiting to launch their books with us. BIRTH. Then there was this blog (that became this book) where I would talk about the stuff in my head that relates to you (and me) and offer writing exercises to help us work our way through life. BIRTH. I have not lost sight of my vision. Yet, I think that the mistakes, blunders, poor choices, poor stewardship and absolutely stupid moves that I was trying to hide were beating that vision down. Therefore, I decided that, "whom the Son sets free is free indeed," and I released all of it. I gave BIRTH to freedom.

I have screwed up! I have had some holes in moneybags (from the Biblical passage)! I did not count all the costs personally, relationally, socially, financially nor spiritually - but unlike Florida during a certain presidential election of note - I have done better in the recount. Still I could not allow the stuff I did not want people to see to continue to block the view INTO MY VISION. I could not continue to see my vision around and through those errors. So I spilled the beans — that is what these reflective words are — me spilling the beans. I screwed up and I wanted to give up because of it, time and time again.

I have wanted to give up. Yet, instead of giving up - I keep getting up and as long as I do I know that everything will be okay. It may not be okay in my time. However, it will be okay. I may get some more nasty emails, harassing letters and text messages and even additional threatening voice mails - but it is okay. All of those things are the remnant of the old creature's habits and that good sister cannot abide in my vision any longer!

So be honest. Haven't you ever wanted to give up? Write down the last three times you have wanted to give up and why. Now pull from the power that is deep inside of you and pull out three great reasons to fight for what you have to offer to this world, your family, your church, your friends and your self that defeat that desire to lay down in the battle.

I messed up some money. Well, yes, you did, but with the abundance you are positioning yourself to receive you will be able to give away double the amount you messed up. *I didn't spend enough time with the kids.* Well, what time is it now? Seems like a good position on the clock to spend time with yours and maybe two others whose parents are working hard to make ends meet. *I didn't honestly do everything I could have on that project.* Still, the next project gives you the opportunity to do more than you ever could have before on any project and it will allow you to mentor someone along the way.

I wanted to give up. I wanted to just lie down and cry. I wanted to wail like a big spoiled baby until God waved His magic wand and made it all go away. It just does not work that way and I am glad it doesn't. While the lessons have been and are hard, (OH BOY THEY ARE HARD), I did not give up. There is a blessed assurance in me that may get rattled, but it will not be defeated. DO NOT GIVE UP!

Write down the last three times you have wanted to give up and why. Now pull from the power that is deep inside of you and pull out three great reasons to fight for what you have to offer to this world:

Today write your future

Oh You are Just Too Excited

In my life's purpose as a writer, editor, literary coach and publisher, I have the privilege of helping people birth books. I call it a privilege because I learn so many wonderful and amazing things from the authors I midwife. What I have found is that what is intended to be a simple literary coaching session often becomes a time of empowerment, introspective reflection, purpose defining and therapy for them and for me. That is so cool! I am also privileged to be able to be on the perimeter watching the dreams of people touch the rising sun. That is something to behold. I will say that with some of my clients, I am often overwhelmed with their excitement. To answer a phone call and a voice has risen two octaves higher or a speech pattern that is normally very deliberate is suddenly fast paced throws me. I get distracted by the excitement and I get so intrigued in it, that the reasons for the excitement are sometimes lost on me.

I get a kick out of the adrenalin and emotion that pulsates through people when they are genuinely and wonderfully excited about something that is happening in their life. That thing - is so absolutely amazing. Life can be so very enchanting and embracing that it urges a typically slightly tenor voice to become more alto-soprano; and a normally mousy personality to giggle loudly like a schoolgirl on the merry-go-round.

I think it is okay to not focus on the reason for the excitement - instead focus on the joy. It is the thing that tickles your spirit - that emotion of contentment - that will hit the ears of someone who has been crying all day and softly dry away their sorrow or discouragement. The reminder of what tears of joy sound like brings a smile to a temporary dark moment; and now there is the thought that I can reach for some of that excitement too. There is sweetness in the belly laugh of achievement that a friend shares with you and I am appreciating the blessing of someone sharing it with me.

There are times when I am sitting in a waiting room at a doctor's office or even in a meeting and I feel a little excitement tickling that spot right behind my navel and right next to my heart. (Yes, I'm sure it's not gas.) When it happens, I cleverly move my hand over my mouth to refrain from just losing it in laughter. I believe that God tickles me from time to time, just to remind me that He wants me to be happy. He wants me to smile. He wants me to be excited about everything that is me. He wants me to laugh at my joy and at my pain, because in both things I am yet alive and able to feel and able to wait for Him to tickle me so I can smile.

God tickles you too. Tell me today in your writing, when was the last time you felt God tickle you? Your tickle may come when you suddenly find a candy bar you haven't seen since you were five (once, for me, it was finding a box of Boston Baked Beans!). Or your tickle may be in a silly joke that keeps playing over and over in your head. Sometimes a tickle can come in those most unusual things that kids say - like when my four year old niece told me that she would not push the skateboard beyond the fence, because, "we don't want to have a situation, right auntie?" (Well okay then!)

There are little tickles that happen in our lives that say you have the right to laugh, to dance, to giggle until you have to run to the bathroom, to cry at the touch of a little one's hand on your face. Write about the tickles you have encountered, smile about them, laugh about them and then rest your head on the Father's chest and tell Him "Thanks, I sure needed that".

Tell me today in your writing, when was the last time you felt God tickle you? Your tickle may come when you suddenly find a candy bar you haven't seen since you were five (once, for me, it was finding a box of Boston Baked Beans!). Or your tickle may be in a silly joke that keeps playing over and over in your head. Write about the tickles you have encountered, smile about them, laugh about them and then rest your head on the Father's chest and tell Him "Thanks, I sure needed that".:

Today write your future

_____

_____

_____

_____

_____

_____

_____

_____

_____

_____

_____

_____

_____

I May not be a Fist-to-Fist Fighter, But I Sure Think Like One

I am not a street fighter. The more accurate statement for me is I really am not a fighting type of person, though I do have a fighter's personality. While in my high temper days I would quickly grab someone – actually hitting them was never necessary. (It is all in the way you grab and look!) Aside from childhood tussles with my sister, I think I have actually only been in maybe three school-aged fights and none as an adult. I mean after all, you do have to grow up at some point.

One fight sticks out in my mind. This girl, (who had been a friend since elementary school), decided one day in eighth grade that we needed to fight. To this day, I do not know why and I do not know if she even offered a reason. When the bell rang for dismal, I and my sister, and our usual crew headed home. This trip however we were accompanied by my sudden new rival, who was taunting me to no end. I ignored her and kept walking. This, I assume, enraged her even more because out of nowhere she produced a knife and told me if I would not fight her, she would cut me. THAT WAS IT!

Books hit the ground. My oversized purse hit the ground. I started beating her like a crazy woman. Then everyone encircled us and our normal walking crew was trying to pull me off of her. There is a certain point though in rage that makes pulling back difficult, if not impossible. My sister was yelling for me to get off of her. Everyone was yelling for me to stop. I do not remember asking myself if I was really inflicting that much damage or if somehow she had in fact managed to cut me and I was bleeding horribly over every crack in the sidewalk.

I do remember my sister finally yelling something about a truck. I had seen the truck heading towards us but still in the distance. In fact, I remember pulling my opponent into the street so that the truck would help me stop her from ever taunting and tormenting me again. My sister was yelling for me to let her go and move, because if the truck hit her it would hit me too. Well, that was not the plan. If I wasn't going to let her cut me, I certainly wasn't going to let her make me get hit by a truck. So I slung her to the other side of the street and when the truck passed, I picked up my purse and my books and walked the rest of the way home.

As I said, physical fights are not my thing. But I do have a fighter's personality. Even when an opponent comes upon them suddenly, a fighting personality will move into a course of action: face the opponent, size them up quickly and get on the offensive, not the defensive in the most feasible and exacting manner – if you take control of the attack you can determine the outcome, or at least force the attack into a more positive outcome for yourself. A true fighter approaches each and every opponent with a winning mindset; being defeated - even if they have never won a bout - is not a possibility.

My life has presented enough battles for me to hone my fighter's personality and has taught me to do whatever I can to strategically and purposely keep my life on the offensive. It takes losing some fights to learn those lessons. It takes getting some foul punches. It takes you initiating some fights that never should have been. It takes you jumping into some fights that were none of your business. It takes you getting a knock out here and there. Nevertheless, developing that fighter's personality also means you condition yourself and you train yourself for the fight. That for me has meant re-aligning my spiritual, emotional and mental thoughts and behavior patterns. Talk about some tough conditioning and training! Yet, I have had to realize that the tangible things that happen in my life could not be purposely designed for my success until I believed with everything in me that they could.

You know I think this kind of training is even harder than the bag, rope and running drills that championship boxers undergo. This is the kind of training that makes you beat down some inside stuff that keeps allowing the outside stuff to knock your behind out. This is the kind of training that will make you stagger but not fall and most importantly keep you punching.

I am KID EC, the HEAVYWEIGHT CHAMPION of my battles. What are you? Who are you? Today, define your fighter. Is he BEATSTREET PAUL or SHANTE THE BRUISER JONES? What is the inside stuff that you finally have to condition and train yourself to defeat? What do you know about the opponents that continue to taunt you? Study them and then get on the offensive, so you can move in victorious circles around the enemy and no matter what the attack, you will be okay. By the way, I am not putting on any of those shiny shorts – oh boy!

Today, define your fighter. Is he BEATSTREET PAUL or SHANTE THE BRUISER JONES? What is the inside stuff that you finally have to condition and train yourself to defeat? What do you know about the opponents that continue to taunt you? Study them and then get on the offensive, so you can move in victorious circles around the enemy:

Today write your future

I am not a Cigarette, So Please Don't Drag on Me

Can I give you a straight up piece of advice that will save you a world of anger, despair and aggravation? Do not waste your time arguing with people who just want to argue, talk and pontificate - the D & D Committee. I personally can't do it. The more they talk, the more characters and story lines I build in my head. Really, I do. I develop story lines based on what I feel their underlying and intrinsic issues are; or, on anything that distracts me from their la la la wah wah wah, can't, ain't, and won't dialogue.

I am occasionally in the presence of someone who often relays stories of people in her life. The thing that strikes me most about these people is their presence in her sphere of being has been long-standing. The second thing that tickles my curiosity is that these people are part of what I call the DRAG and DESPAIR COMMITTEE. This is the committee of people that will drag on you with consistent negativity about your life, consistent negativity and bad news about their life, about what you want to do, about suggestions to have fun, about ANY and EVERY thing.

For me, the blocking out of the blah blah blah and wah wah wah of such unproductive and dragging dialogue is my defense mechanism for that immediate moment. It is the way I teach myself patience and not to speak in what might be considered a rude or sarcastic manner. (Because I can be both) In a medium range and more permanent nature, I will eventually sit down and ask myself some questions.

Am I now dragging on other people by relaying stories of the drag and despair committee member?

Is there something that I can lend positively and constructively to Miss or Mr. Drag?

Should I consider whether or not their season of importance in my life has changed?

Do I imply that there is an open invitation to drag me down with the practices of the committee, by never saying - I would like to talk to you about why your words and conversations are always such a drag?

Is my life going to be negatively or positively impacted if I close the door on this perpetual negative energy and instead replace it with life, hope and power?

In the interim, until you finally get to the point where you are either going to pull every single strand of hair from your head one at a time, or have the conversation above with yourself - try these things. First and foremost - be quiet. Stop giving the drag and despair committee information about your circumstances. Second - separate. One of the most profound statements I have ever read in the Bible (Joshua 7:13) says simply, "remove thyself from the accursed thing." If it is dragging you down in any way, it is pretty safe to say it is a curse. There is entirely too much bitterness, negativity and demoting of one's spirit for there not to be. Third - get out of familiar territory. You may just need to get a new group of positive people to enjoy and do life with; who can impart wisdom, promote your vision and just hang out with you in love. Fourth - interrogate yourself based on the questions above and be serious. Just because he or she has been a friend for 20 years; does not mean their impact on your life needs to be as great as it is.

Here is what I want you to do while you are still highly interactive with the drag and despair committee member; as they talk, write a note to yourself, advising you to cease from pointless conversations, not to waste other's time with mindless words of confusion. Write a reason to say something productive to everyone you encounter. Productivity breeds productivity.

The other thing I have found about D & D committee members is that they are often the people first in line during my day – and probably yours too. They want to argue, they always want to talk about why I am wrong and they are right, they always want to tell someone else what they think I said and what they feel about what they really did not hear. Tragically, before you know it, you will mimic them in the words you speak and the spirit you emanate. You have unwittingly become the newest member of the DRAG and DESPAIR COMMITTEE. So, write a little note to the arguer, saying something as simple as – "I appreciate your energy, maybe next time it won't interfere with my understanding of what you were trying to relay or on my invitation for you to enjoy living and life."

Above all remember this, you are not a cigarette so do not allow these people to drag on you - otherwise you will become mashed up and squeezed down into the bottom of an ashtray. Are you not so much more than that?

Here is what I want you to do while you are still highly interactive with the drag and despair committee member; as they talk, write a note to yourself, advising you to cease from pointless conversations, not to waste other's time with mindless words of confusion. Write a reason to say something productive to everyone you encounter. Productivity breeds productivity:

Today write your future

_____

_____

_____

_____

_____

_____

_____

_____

_____

_____

_____

_____

_____

_____

_____

Affirm Your Life

I have adopted affirming my life as a way of life. It has done wonders for the transformation of my emotional, intellectual and spiritual being. I certainly need those three things aligned to God and the positive energy that circulates around us. You see, I understand completely that their health is directly tied to my ability to exist in peace and rest in the true nature of God. Therefore, I have learned to affirm, speak and claim every powerful and positive thing I need to manifest in my life.

Interestingly, when I worked for a gospel station, I (and some others on staff) would often tease the midday host about a particular song she would play as she closed out a special prayer segment. In a weird kind of way, a strange piano key would be played at just the right moment as she read a particular scripture. So enthralled in the music and teasing her about it, I missed the power of that scriptural passage for years. It says: whatsoever things are true, whatsoever things are honest, whatsoever things are just, whatsoever things are pure, whatsoever things are lovely, whatsoever things are of good report; if there be any virtue, and if there be any praise, think on these things (Philippians 4:8). It is about affirming.

I can raise my hand along with many of you at this statement - life has some hard, difficult, bad and painful days. A medical diagnosis, a broken marriage, a sudden death, or a child bent on doing everything that pleases hell, can register like an earthquake of unbelievable proportions in our lives. Yet that are some true, honest, pure, lovely and just things that we can infuse into every situation to squash the negative and damaging energy that comes with hard moments. *I am healed. I am whole in spite of who has walked out of my life. I am complete in me and my God. I am perfectly positioned to accept the provision that is for me. I am confident that my child is safe and that no manner of evil will overtake him. I am true and unconditional love and therefore true and unconditional love is all that will come into my life.*

You have to affirm some things daily in your life. There are times my affirmations may change. I have learned to use them as weapons in my arsenal for holistic success and achievement. That means I believe and accept that the words are more than just flowery statements. They are in fact, marching orders. I speak them and they go out and get what I speak. What are you speaking into your life today? What are you speaking about the hard challenges that shake you awake in the middle of the night? Are your words giving life to the challenges or giving life to the positive resolution of the same?

What can you affirm that speaks directly to what your life needs, right now? Write your affirmations. I will help you get started:

I am all things light. Where there is light, there is no darkness.
I am powerfully positioned to bless others.
I am forgiving and I am forgiven.
I hold no anger in my heart or spirit. I release it so that I can receive love.

Above all things know that what you speak is what will happen in your being and in everything connected to it. If you are going to talk, how about this: speak life, speak peace, speak joy, speak affirming words - otherwise be sure that you can live abundantly in what you say.

You have to affirm some things daily in your life. I have learned to use them as weapons in my arsenal for holistic success and achievement. Write your affirmations. I will help you get started: I am all things light. Where there is light, there is no darkness:

Today write your future

_____

_____

_____

_____

_____

_____

_____

_____

_____

_____

_____

_____

_____

_____

_____

_____

God Tones are - Well - Not to be Ignored

Do you ever get instructions from God? Some may call them signs from the universe. Since I believe in the resurrected Christ - for me, they are instructions or little understandings from God. I have often received "God Tones" over a period of time and have learned to jot them down. When I go back and read them after several days or weeks - they carry a powerful message.

In my wonderful ability to sometimes be on the short bus in spite of the obvious - I have missed this important knowledge about the purpose of God Tones- God was giving me foresight to my coming experience! Oh, wow! How I wish I could go back and hear and apply the God Tones in different seasons over the years. I am more sensitive to them now. I pray for clarity and understanding in them and I watch for the life occurrence that corresponds.

I remember a string of God Tones in 2009 that gave me goose bumps. Those tones said: release dead things, get out of familiar territory, prepare a place for Me to bless you, and no matter the attack listen for my still voice. The tones were clear and definitive messages on how to bring a new and comprehensively focused order to my life. So key were these God Tones that a unique confidence sprouted in my spirit. This is the confidence that comes from moments of darkness and the pains of desiring divine promises. It is a sincere confidence. It is an it-is-well-with-my-soul confidence.

What God Tones or universal signs have you heard? Today draw and write with me. Adorn yourself in the words of life just for you. Draw a necklace of pearls. In each pearl write a God Tone that has tickled your mind's ears. When you are done, you will notice that you are blessed with road signs indicating where you are at this moment or a code of conduct for the moments fast approaching. God Tones do not make the journey easier, but they do provide guidance and blessed assurance. What are you hearing?

Today draw and write with me. Adorn yourself in the words of life just for you. Draw a necklace of pearls. In each pearl write a God Tone that has tickled your mind's ears. When you are done, you will notice that you are blessed with road signs indicating where you are at this moment or a code of conduct for the moments fast approaching:

Today write your future

_____

_____

_____

_____

_____

_____

_____

_____

_____

_____

_____

_____

_____

_____

Child, I Got Me a Gift

A dear friend said to me that my gift, the thing that I am good at is BIRTHING. Not in a having babies giving birth kind of way - but in a birthing dreams and untapped vision kind of way. Her response to a question I posed threw me for a loop, yet confirmed something within me. My question to her, "What do you believe I am really good at and on what should focus my energy?"

What threw me in her response was the knowledge that someone else saw it clearly enough to put it into words. Several other things came back to my conscious state when she shared her thoughts with me. One - that a woman who has never given birth naturally would be so gifted. Two - that in a time of prayer, a minister said to me that my womb (though I had undergone a hysterectomy) would be prepared for birth again. Three - when the minister spoke those words, I had not shared that I had never given birth from my natural womb, the hysterectomy or my unwavering belief that I was at a point in my life where I was unable to birth spiritually, professionally or creatively. Yet, three years later, a friend would recognize the same thing the minister did in me - BIRTH.

The challenge for me is accepting the power of my gift. Surely accepting and recognizing your gift and then accepting its power is a challenge for you as well. Each time I sit with a coaching client, I ask that God give me wisdom and guidance. I believe that every thing we write has the capacity to be therapeutic and therefore I do not take their work or mine for granted. While they do not understand my methods or lines of questioning (and often I am clueless too); it all, I have discovered, is more about the author than the story. I cannot explain why it is that way; but I do know that giving birth is a process. It is a process that requires the mother to be as healthy as possible for the nurturing and ultimate delivery of the life within her. The doctor or midwife facilitates the components that make up the birthing process and they all work together to give birth. So I am honored to have a gift for birthing. I am equally and wonderfully intimidated about how I should unwrap and offer this gift.

So what is the gift you must now unwrap and offer? Imagine that you have been given a box. Inside this box, your gift has been carefully and lovingly placed. The box was then beautifully decorated with colorful wrapping, flowing ribbons and curly bows. There is a card attached that says, "Do not open until this gift makes room for you." The note also says, "The gift is not for you but for the edifying of others."

What is in your box and in whose presence will you open it? Maybe it is the gift of song or the gift of deciphering dreams - whatever it is recognize it, respect it and use it to the benefit of others. Then you will experience how awesome being gifted really is.

... what is the gift you must now unwrap and offer? Imagine that you have been given a box. Inside this box, your gift has been carefully and lovingly placed. The box was then beautifully decorated with colorful wrapping, flowing ribbons and curly bows. There is a card attached that says, "Do not open until this gift makes room for you." The note also says, "The gift is not for you but for the edifying of others:

Today write your future

The Man the Good Samaritan Helped

There is a Biblical story with which many of us - Christian or not- are familiar. It is the story of the Good Samaritan. The story, in brief, is about a Jewish man beaten and left in a ditch, and who is overlooked deliberately by two religious men. A supposed natural enemy of his, a Samaritan, comes by and rescues him and attends to his wounds. During a personal time of study, I became fascinated by the man in the ditch. He was attacked by thieves, stripped of his clothing, thrown in a ditch and left to die. I imagine that because he was not dead - there were moments of consciousness where he probably thought to, tried to, or even did cry out. Why my fascination with this man in the ditch? I have been much like him. Except my thieves have been lingering negative and defeating mindsets. I know many others that have been this man in the ditch and we just could not get out of that hole by the roadside on our journey.

Because I believe I did not dig deep enough into self during my periodic life detoxification periods, these defeating programs were very present and very active. So my inner thieves, particularly in a major area of my life had stripped me of a significant part of my integrity, my faith in God, my belief in myself and in my ability to position myself for success. Many of us are the man in the ditch - not because of what others did to us - but because of our bad decisions, emotional decisions, and decisions without wise counsel.

When we do not pay attention to the subtle and often loud warnings, we become both victim and perpetrator. We end up in a self-created ditch and even worse, we get major attitude when someone passes us and ignores us. Frustrated, filled with pride and ashamed - our cries for help grow quiet and sit wearily in our spirits until something pushes them up and out. We release our pride and release our requests for help and a step out of the ditch is underway.

Make a decision today to come out of your ditch. Write a brief story about how you ended up in the ditch; then take action. With every WHY in the story - list a HOW you can overcome that WHY. Now challenge yourself - set a realistic goal date to succeed in overcoming step by step. I say realistic goal date because we tend to put ourselves back in a ditch when we set a goal (in example) to get out of 25 thousand dollars in debt in three months. We then commit to something that is not feasible or intelligent. Most importantly, take your eyes off of who has and who is passing you by as you wallow in your ditch. Instead, focus on this - there is a Samaritan who will finally come along and provide compassion, according to what he/she is able to do and according to what you really need.

Write a brief story about how you ended up in the ditch; then take action. With every WHY in the story - list a HOW you can overcome that WHY. Now challenge yourself - set a realistic goal date to succeed in overcoming step by step:

Today write your future

Listen – Before you Need a Recovery Plan

My life yelled at me. Baby!!! It yelled in a loud, distinct and unmistakable manner. It said - there is failure before greatness, there are valleys before greatness, there are problems before greatness and in every measure of anticipated and expected success there are measures of well - hell - to walk through. Can I let you in on a little secret? My life, in hindsight, probably had been whispering the things it started yelling - but I'm a little hard of hearing in my left ear and I am prone to being stubborn. My mother will tell you that of her three children, I am the most stubborn. Here is the thing - life has no respect of stubbornness. If I were a charismatic Baptist preacher, I would say - "Oh y'all don't hear me. I said life has no respect of stubbornness."

Since it does not, life and God will wait you out until they get tired of you. I mean really, God owns time and life; you cannot wait Him out. I admit I have tried. Silly silly me. When my life yelled, and I was forced to listen, I realized I had some things that needed to be worked out. There were some things attached to the way and the reasons I do/did things that I had not recognized. For example, the majority of my financial decisions were made from a place of desperation; therefore my finances have always hit crisis mode several times during the year. Life screamed it and I had to deal with the chastisement of not handling that reality while it was yet a whisper. I began to speak a powerful dream over myself, not realizing that dreams are often manifested through major battles; yet that does not mean the dream is deferred or denied. Life screamed it and I realized

I should have paid attention to the warnings to be quiet now or speak now that would stir in my spirit.

When life gets to the point that it has to scream at you, you will find that it will also tell you to get a recovery plan. You will find yourself like major financial institutions and the auto industry - looking for a bailout. Guess what? It may not come raining down from heaven and it may not be a plausible solution that people around you will help you with. You may just have to bail yourself out and do some things to enter into a new level of humility. Your life may effectively tell you that a bail out plan to make you an excellent manager of every area of your life is now necessary and urgent.

If you could see me now you would see my hand is raised for I am so there. While the God I serve is so able to send one person into my life to address the pressing need for emergency money - He has not. While the Bible says money answer all things (Ecclesiastes 10:19), what needed answering for me is not the things that need money, but the actions and mindsets that created the need. I am not being favored with cash, but favored with understanding. While the God I love is more than able to speak healing into my body - He has not. By His stripes I am surely healed; but, I am healed even more when I recognize that this temple was given to me for a reason and what I experience in it is for a bigger purpose. Since it is, I am being favored with a new respect for it and a renewed desire to live.

Life said, "Ms. Thing, get a bailout plan so that you can get exceedingly, abundantly, above all you can ask for." That means making some decisions that bring tears to my eyes. That means having and working through brief moments of feeling like a failure. That means letting go of and returning some material things that no longer fit. That means being uncomfortable in my lifestyle in order to become comfortable in my life - before it yells at me again.

Take a look at your life areas: money, health, family, spirit, and professional/business. Does your life need a bailout plan? Is your life headed towards needing a bailout plan? Are you missing the whispers and inviting life to YELL? In every significant area of your life write one distinct vision and one pivotal question - is my life following my vision in this area? If not, a life bailout plan is in order.

What goes into your bailout plan depends on your vision, therefore discuss it with God and with one person who knows your sincere spirit (and God's) and will be honest with you. This plan is about what your life is showing you and not what others think about what you should do in your life - being mindful of that is vital. In a country where large corporate bailouts became as normal as pulling through a fast food drive thru - now is the perfect time to re-order a slice of life that is effective, feasible and divinely blessed. Grab a bucket and start bailing out some things, because when life yells, it is deafening.

In every significant area of your life write one distinct vision and one pivotal question - is my life following my vision in this area? If not, a life bailout plan is in order. What goes into your bailout plan depends on your vision, therefore discuss it with God and with one person who knows your sincere spirit (and God's) and will be honest with you:

Today write your future

I Have a Love Jones for Me

I received a rather scathing email one day. My decisions on some things had clearly perplexed the beliefs of someone else. One line in that email disturbed me more than every other word listed. That line reported that my problem is I don't love myself. Wow! What a hard thing to say to someone! What an untrue statement about me. Five years ago, ten years ago - in high school - that statement would have been a glaring and blinding reality. I probably wore it like a theatre marquee over my head, DOES NOT LOVE HERSELF. I learned to love me by learning to walk through my experiences and pull what could make me better, wiser, stronger and more enlightened from each of them.

So why did the statement in the email bother me? It reminded me that I have not totally moved into loving me completely. I still occasionally take a step back when my life and my decisions offend those close to me. I still occasionally feel guilty about doing little things or great things for myself because of the criticism of others. I still occasionally allow the glares, comments and opinions about the extra pounds and what I do with them, to make me feel like the little fat girl in Ms. Liotti's fourth grade class. I still occasionally, (though I consciously fight it now), put on boxing gloves and pound myself about things that I really have no control over and are not mine to fix or ponder. I do love me. I love my crazy long toenails, my fat fingers that look like stubs when my nails are short. I love my big ears. I love the gift of writing that graces my life. I love this tapping into my inner self and releasing it.

I do love me and today I say to me that it is really okay to consciously love me totally and unconditionally first. That kind of self-love will certainly teach me to love my son on a deeper level and my God as well. The really great thing is when I learned to love me - I also learned how to get unloving relationships or relationships where love was secondary out of my life. You know what I think? I think aside from parents and children, no other human vessel should pull more love from you than the love you have for yourself. God gives you the ability and the reasons to love you and anything and anyone that discounts that - should be approached with caution.

I do love me - the me that I am today and all of the variations of me I have been over the years. I love the fat girl in elementary school on whom the kids picked. I love the smart fat girl in high school who the guys respected but would not date. I love the young woman who purposely dated married men because I didn't think I could do any better. I love the professional woman that walked away from a job when I was told to choose between that position and being a new mom. I love the professional woman that went back to that job until it was clear there was nothing that I could contribute because it was time for me to move into what I had been praying for. I love the Christian woman who has realized that God is a hard man to love, because we want to define how He should love us based on our temporary and seasonal conditions. Yet, God is the ultimate right man to love. I love the patient woman facing hard medical conditions and believing none of it is unto death and I will be healed. I love the maternal woman who has learned how a hug from a little body, my Lord, can make up for all the hell that comes against you. I do love me.

The truth of the matter is I haven't written a love letter to myself in quite some time. You have to write letters of love and adoration to yourself every now and then. You should do this, on the surface, as a reminder of just how fabulous you are; but more importantly, to continue to evolve into a loving, loveable and in love with self, kind of person. No one can love someone who has no love for self. For loving self creates respect, esteem, vision, power and purpose. Will you do something for me? Write the most intimate, moving words of love to yourself - today. Let your words love on you, love you through the hard moments, love you until you cry out in the sheer joy of who you are. Look up. What does the marquee over your head flash? I am thrilled to say my marquee now reads: LOVING ME NOW AND LOVING ME BETTER.

You have to write letters of love and adoration to yourself every now and then. You should do this, on the surface, as a reminder of just how fabulous you are; but more importantly, to continue to evolve into a loving, loveable and in love with self, kind of person. Write the most intimate, moving words of love to yourself - today:

Today write your future

Go Ahead, Get on the Plane

One summer, (I believe it was 2009 or 2010), I was blessed with an opportunity to facilitate a writing workshop at the East Point Georgia Public Library. I had a great time and had the opportunity to reconnect with a friend I had not seen in years. When she took me to the airport for my flight home, I was so focused on the fact that I had everything I needed with me that I did not check for any flight changes. When I approached the gate listed on the boarding pass (as the flight was boarding), I was told the flight to Ft. Lauderdale had been moved to the other side of Hartsfield airport. As I headed to the new gate, I ran into a woman I met moments prior on the train to the gates and told her our flight had been changed. We decided to put our names on standby after realizing we were not going to make the new flight and customer service said they would not hold it. She paused and said her kids live close to the airport and she thought it best to just call them and have them come back. For some reason I stepped into what was not my decision and convinced her to do otherwise. Long story short, she got on the next flight and I ended up spending the night in a deserted airport and not flying out until the next morning. Unlike her, everyone I know in the area lives at least 50 miles from the airport and I couldn't see having them drive to get me and then bring me back at 5am.

Fast forward about a month after that incident, I had a succession of dreams. In the first, a younger female and I were to catch a plane. We realized that we were going to be rushed to get to the airport. I panicked but she said to me, "My father has already taken care of all of our stuff there." In an instant, we were at the airport and could hear announcements for us to get to our gates. We ran through one door and a woman said, "You can't go through there you are too late." The young woman and I suddenly got separated and I found myself back at an entrance. The announcements for my name began again, "Passenger Claudette Freeman please report to your gate immediately for your flight." I tried to go through the gate again - Gate 7, but was told my flight was not there. I had to get to Gate 17. As I turned around to run there, there was an airport worker driving a couple of other people to another gate and I jumped aboard the cart to go to Gate 17, which was literally right next to the gate where I was standing - yet I did not notice it until I got off the cart.

I approached the ticket counter and said, "You all have been paging me, I guess I was in the wrong place."

She said, "What is your name?"

I responded, "You have been paging Claudette Freeman, but as you see from my ID, the first name is really Emily."

She smiled, "Oh, no problem. The flight has not left, but I'm not sure it is still on the runway near the terminal, we will have to get you on board another way."

She and I walked to the runway and she turned to me and said, "Just wait a moment the pilot is going to move forward a little and then you can board." Then she looked at me very calmly, smiled and said, "You know this flight would have waited for you without you rushing to get here. All you needed to do is call." I looked at her and thought that doesn't make sense - why would the flight wait for me and why didn't I get on the flight at the first gate?

In the second airport dream, I was with a cousin. We were walking towards the gates when a woman pages me, "Emily Freeman report to gate 17 for boarding." This time, I walked towards the gate and in this process; I again got separated from my companion. I asked the girl at the counter if I was supposed to be at gate 17- she said, "Yes ma'am."

I asked, "But the woman I'm traveling with, this isn't her gate?"

She responded. "No, this point is for gate 16 and gate 17 travelers only." I walked through Gate 17 headed for the plane.

In the third airport dream, I was alone and this time I actually looked at the ticket in my hand realizing it was some type of all or special access pass. I walked up to the ticket counter and the agent told me my connecting flight would not leave until nine that night. I asked if there was a direct flight to Ft. Lauderdale.

She checked and responded, "Yes it leaves at 6:35."

I decided to take that one instead. Then she told me, she didn't believe I could use the pass for the earlier flight. She walked away to talk to a supervisor, who then called me over and advised me that the pass would work. He explained to the young lady that she was looking for information about my pass from the general information page and not the main system page - the pass is good for all flights. I turned around after saying thanks to walk off towards the gate.

God taught me some very crucial and challenging things for women (and men as well) destined to do more than average in these dreams.

1) When God is shifting, moving, preparing you for takeoff you need to learn to mind your own business. We often get so focused on making sure everyone is where we want them to be and how we want them to be, that we move ourselves out of God's way and plan.

2) Check the ticket in your hand. There is a reason you are flying out of one gate and others around you, even those that you have cried with, prayed with, and relied on have different gate numbers. Where you are going is predestined for you - not them. Know that it is okay to allow them to take their appointed flight without you as well.

3) Don't get comfortable in what you know, I had done all the advance stuff, I had no bags to check and I printed my boarding pass earlier that day. It never occurred to me to check for flight changes. I was comfortable in the knowledge that I had taken care of everything and yet my flight plans were altered and delayed.

4) In the season of preparing for a dimensional shift, don't readily accept the first report or answer you receive, instead take it before the Father; perhaps the initial response came from general information and not the divine main source.

5) Pay attention to where you are in God's process. What God has for you could potentially be closer than you think.

Then God illuminated two other vital things in these dreams. The tickets or passes in my hand on each of these flights, gave me access to flights that would not leave without me. Whether you travel inadvertently or deliberately away from His assignment, know this Jonah, His Will - will absolutely be done in your life and His purpose will absolutely manifest in you when it is ordained for you. The other key thing, that brought me to tears, is even with all of the access, and the assurance shown to me in each of these dreams and in God's Word, I never actually saw myself board or take off on either of those flights, and it was not God delaying or denying the next steps - it was me.

Not boarding those flights came from a place of not trusting the greatness and gifting that God put in me. Nor did I trust the spiritual knowledge that the delicately rough season of preparation and pruning I was being blessed to learn from - was actually going to lead to something amazing as promised in The Word. I, in the midst of one thing after another, diverted my focus from Jeremiah 29:11, "For I know the plans I have for you," declares the LORD, "plans to prosper you and not to harm you, plans to give you hope and a future." I was comfortable and conditioned with simply going to the next level, when God is a God of dimensions, realms and territories.

My faith in the God in me, said, "Oh you can handle walking through the gate – but you're not ready to take flight." In hindsight, I realized that when I stepped away from radio, by faith, in 2007, I stepped into my gate or talent (writing) – but God called me to move into my gifting or dimension, which is counseling and helping others birth their vision. I, however, thought, He can't be calling me. Yet prophetic word after prophetic word confirmed it and finally, I got the picture. That picture is wonderfully painted in First John 4, verse 15,

"Whosoever shall confess that Jesus is the Son of God, God dwelleth in him, and he in God." The dwelling power of God in me, is my all access pass to what He has already prepared and purposed for my life. I have to trust the indwelling and board the flight.

I believe I have finally stepped on that flight. I have started to come out of the background, where I excelled and said, "God if the all access pass in my hand is about my life touching another then so be it." It is a bit unnerving, exciting and altogether lovely. Will you write your ticket or all access pass to your flight? What will you put in words to give yourself permission to board the flight, as opposed to putting yourself on standby? Have you considered that you might be stranded in the airport, when there is a pilot and a flight waiting for you before it can take off?

When I was a young girl, actress Sally Field played the role of The Flying Nun in a TV show; no matter the challenge, this nun would simply take flight towards a potential solution. Are you bold enough to simply take flight believing that God is truly the wind beneath your wings? Can you be confident in knowing that the Master Pilot has a flight plan just for you? Can you trust that He is able to send angels in various forms to accompany you to your destination? Can you trust the God in you enough to finally realize just how powerful it is to have an all access pass in your hand, and step into a new yet unfamiliar dimension and board your flight? Can you really grasp and embrace Isaiah 40:31 as the living power for your life: "But those who trust in the LORD will find new strength. They will soar high on wings like eagles. They will run and not grow weary. They will walk and not faint." Your flight attendants are waiting – are you ready to fly?

Can you trust the God in you enough to finally realize just how powerful it is to have an all access pass in your hand, and step into a new yet unfamiliar dimension and board your flight?:

Today write your future

_____

_____

_____

_____

_____

_____

_____

_____

_____

_____

_____

_____

_____

_____

_____

Dreamer get on Board – The Plane is Here

In the preceding pages, I shared with you a series of airport dreams to which I was divinely privy to. This time I want to share with you a fourth airport dream. I decided to share them back to back because I believe one series of lessons leads to another; and combined there is a powerful strategy that comes from the Master Life Coach – God. In this fourth dream, I had been sitting at the airport for quite some time waiting for my flight, not really concerned with the time or anything. Suddenly something said look at the ticket in your hand. When I did, I realized my flight, which I thought had not taken off, had actually departed about 7 that morning. I had missed the flight.

I went to the ticket counter for the respective airline and when I approached the counter, I recognized the woman working there and she recognized me. I said, "I thought I was early for my flight, but it left this morning."

She asked if I wanted to change it and explained that changing a ticket is not usually what they do, so I would probably have to buy a new one. Then she smiled and whispered that since it was me, she would see what she could do. I turned away from the counter for just a second, and when I turned back, another young woman and a man were there. The man, like the first woman, recognized me and I seemed to be comfortable with or have some knowledge of him.

He said, "We can change this ticket, but it may cost you something." He printed out something and handed it to me, indicating the cost to change the ticket.

There was an astronomical cost on the printout - like 11 thousand dollars or something.

Of course, I said, "I can't pay that!"

He then said, "Let me see what I can do for you." Once again he printed out something and the second printout read $75; which was the precise amount I had in my hand. I paid him; he gave me a receipt and then offered to walk over to the gate with me.

As we walked over to the gates, I realized I had a receipt but no boarding pass, and so naturally, I asked him for it. He said, in a very matter-of-fact tone, "don't worry about it;" but he still sent the young lady back to get it. We entered one door which led to a well-lit pathway where several people were milling around. Strangely, a woman offered me a piece of fruit, and I took it just as the other young woman reappeared. Still, I was not handed a boarding pass, and so I inquire again.

He then touched a bag on his shoulder and said, "Don't worry I have your pass right here." We then entered another door that revealed what appeared to be a waiting room.

In this waiting room, I immediately recognized the face of a woman I used to work with, and she saw me, yet we did not interact with each other. The guy opened the hatch to the plane, and said, "it's time to board." I started to ascend the stairs to the plane, but it was uncomfortable because the stairs were steep and in fact, I hit one of my knees on one of them and thought, "this is painful maybe I should climb down." I looked back and as quickly as I did – I decided in my conscious thought realm to get on this plane! And so, I did. The problem was, while dreams are typically in the subconscious; I had become so aware consciously of what was happening that I excitedly woke myself. I was excited because after three other related dreams where planes and plans were made, altered and held for me, I never boarded the flights. THIS TIME I had finally gotten on the plane!

I thought about why I had not noticed the time on the ticket. I am a person that prides herself on being prompt and time conscious, but I slipped up. While the

Bible clearly tells us in Philippians 4:12 to "know what it is to be in need, and I know what it is to have plenty. I have learned the secret of being content in any and every situation, whether well fed or hungry, whether living in plenty or in want." We still have to remember that the New Testament in Ephesians 3: 20 also reminds us that He "is able to do exceedingly abundantly above all that we can ask or think according to the power that works in us." The Spirit reminded me to pay attention to the message in your hand, on the wall and in front of you. Don't get so comfortable sitting in your situation and in your waiting that you miss the fact that God has a set time for you to move/shift/transition; and more importantly do not miss the fact that He is moving and bringing some things to pass.

Lesson 1 from this dream – pay attention to God's timing so that you know when to respond urgently within the power working in you.

My mind then went to the whole matter at the counter with the woman I knew, and the man of whom I was aware. She knew me and she knew that there was an assignment to which I needed to get to. She was in place to assure that what needed to be done for me was in fact done. Know then, that God will put people where you are, to help you get to the place to which you are going. She was in place to help me on my journey. When she could not perform the full task - without my asking - God put someone in her place that could produce the results that would match what was in my hand – so that I could keep going.

Lesson 2 – Even if you miss your original flight, God still has people with the provision and resources in place to help you, or to get you to those who can verify and respond positively and properly to your anointing.

Now, there was the matter of the girl I once worked with seated in the waiting area and while we made eye contact, there was no interaction. God said to me that there are some that will always be in waiting because they are not bold enough to take two steps to get to the plane. I realized that I could have done one of two things at that moment. I could have sat down and become distracted in conversation and gossip about what used to be or I could have boarded that plane. In your season of boarding, know that it is detrimental to look back, to go back, and to re-address the old. Do not get distracted – get on your flight. Then I remembered, being stranded in Atlanta. God opened my eyes to something and then immediately told me, "Don't be upset, it was a lesson you needed to learn." While the woman I met probably did not do it intentionally, she was placed on standby first, and although she was aware that I needed to get home to my son, that I really did not have the availability to stay in Atlanta like she did - when the ticket agent said, "either of you can go, it's up to you all." She took the flight.

Well, I thought okay, what is the lesson in that beyond mind your own business?

Lesson 3 is stop reserving space in your life for unfamiliar, unnecessary or unsettling spirits and people while you are approaching your flight. There are some people who are sent to distract, delay and deny your passage to the next level and you must not allow them to be successful. For, the A clause of John 10:10 warns us that the thief's purpose is "to steal and kill and destroy." Just because it seems small and harmless doesn't mean it cannot wreak havoc.

In my dissecting of these dreams, I then came to those stairs. Those stairs hurt my big brown thighs on that climb up, and even in the dream when I saw them, I heard myself say, "Oh this is not going to be a pretty climb." Then to hit my knee – oh it was not a fun climb to board that plane. Can I tell you a lesson that I have fought against learning, cried about learning, said to God why do I have to get it this way (with my spoiled self) – ascension is not always easy, normal or without pain. Your climb to board your flight may be unusual; it may be so steep that it hurts. You may take some hits; but you have got to board the plane.

Understand something else that is very important to your witness. If you look behind you or even next to you, there are others who cannot board or may potentially be delayed if you try to descend when you are supposed to be ascending. You have been gifted with the responsibility to care for the spirit and soul of someone else. Even on the cross, while His body was overwhelmed with pain and agony, Jesus gave charge to John to see to His mother's well being. His ascension was for her. You must ascend because you have that unusual gift inside that will not settle and will not rest until you get to a higher level. That gift is tired of responding and settling to fear and it is fighting, for it knows the words of Romans 8:15a, "For you have not received a spirit of slavery that leads you into fear again." There is a message in your life, in your pain, in your steep and difficult climb that others are waiting to hear. They are sitting in that waiting room, looking for you to take your flight. There is an important thing I forgot to mention about the gentleman supervisor. He never handed me my boarding pass, instead he boarded before me and watched as I made the climb. He was protecting the mission assigned to me while he walked with me, because the thief was close to us. He lurked in a familiar face in a waiting room hoping he could distract me.

Lesson 4 - Stretch your faith, knowing that there are mighty wings shielding you as you are guided to a new dimension.

Still the steep stairs kept taunting me. Why, I asked God, if I am doing what you called me out to do, is the climb so difficult? Why couldn't I be one of those people you hear about who stepped out on faith and seemed to just step into oh such wonderful favor and did not seem to go through anything? Why are my stairs so steep?

Jesus endured some severe things on the way to crucifixion – which for those who accused Him was His just punishment – but for those who love Him, we know now it was the greatest ascension. While in His holding pattern on the cross, He endured the taunts, the loud mouths and when He merely asked for water, He was given sour wine with hyssop on a sponge. Yet when He had died His physical death, His spirit life and our victory was beginning. When Mary saw Jesus at the tombs, He said, "I have not yet ascended to my Father, but I have risen from the dead." So the lessons of the steep stairs from dream four that took me to the story of the crucifixion, resurrection and pending ascension of Christ are these:

Lesson 5 - There is some death from which you need to arise. There has to be death of mindsets, shaky beliefs and rampant self-doubt, because they all say that there is no power and no purpose in you – and that is a lie that you can no longer carry on your shoulders. This is your day to unwrap your tomb clothing. There are some inner conflicts that you have been having with *your* spirit and

The Spirit, that have to die. I would ask this question, if the Spirit is not calling you to something more, then whom do you keep saying no to? I would then ask, if you keep crying out for something and the Spirit keeps saying, "I'm here," why not let Him be what and who you need? I had some inner junk that had to die. You see, I wanted and expected whatever I asked of God to happen the way I wanted and expected it to happen. I had a problem with being spoiled and God had to show me that He had a problem with it too, so He dealt with it and I took another step up that steep climb. I had to sit down with God one morning over a cup of tea for Him to reveal to me that I get disillusioned too easily with the process and preparation for greatness. I get disillusioned when it doesn't snap, crackle and pop just so and I step back. I step back into wanting to flourish in the background. I step back into feeling as if I am not good enough and have nothing to share; and when God keeps pushing me forward – I say God this can't be for me. I had to nail it to the cross and leave it there.

Lesson 6 – Understand that what you are going through and what you have been through is not only for your ascension but for the ascension of others – you have a destiny to carry the weight of death on your shoulders, but give the gift of encouragement, empowerment and life through the fact that when you inhale this second and when you exhale in the next second, you are alive and life must come from you.

Lesson 7 – Before you get to your ultimate destination, you need to get up and talk to somebody and let them know you are alive. The testimonial power for them comes in knowing that you have lived; even though the actors, the enemies, the thieves, the doubters and even the enemy within, taunted you during the most difficult parts of your journey. Remember this, through condemnation and torture Jesus still ascended – after He made it clear that death could not kill Him. While our physical bodies will surely one day succumb, there is no mental, professional, intellectual or psychological death that you cannot rise from and then tell someone looking for you in the tombs – I have not ascended yet, but I ain't dead either.

Will you dare yourself to write what is on each of those steep stairs that encourages you to continue to ascend? With each step, what is the power you gain? Who has gone before you or whom can you trust to go ahead of you to intercede for you against the enemy as you ascend? Can you trust this person to guard your boarding pass knowing that the all access pass in your hand is only for you? Have you taken a look at the ticket lately to see when you need to board your flight? God has put purpose, power and potential in your very body and it must come forth, God is calling it out today, as He called Lazarus from the grave. This is the season for the peculiar of us, to arise. Our flight attendants are on guard, our help is waiting, our course is planned – though the journey to the flight has been hard, though we have been rejected by some and laughed at by others, though there are some who see the greatness in and on us that we do not see and have tried to alter it. Though we have tarried when we should have moved urgently – we are not forsaken by the One who predestined us before conception. Moreover, because we are not forsaken – we can and we must ascend because of the Father and the power of His Spirit within.

The Spirit reminded me to pay attention to the message in your hand, on the wall and in front of you. Will you dare yourself to write what is on each of those steep stairs that encourages you to continue to ascend? With each step, what is the power you gain? Who has gone before you or whom can you trust to go ahead of you to intercede for you against the enemy as you ascend?:

Today write your future

_____

_____

_____

_____

_____

_____

_____

_____

_____

_____

_____

_____

_____

_____

_____

_____

My Design, My Style, My Me

I have come to the conclusion that I am a prime candidate for one of those HGTV (Home and Garden Television) design shows. Honestly! I know what I like and I know the colors that speak to me (that sounds real artsy - right?) I think that my home, if designed according to my spirit and desires, would be a design enigma. Nothing would rhyme. Instead, everything would be an independent story. Turquoise would dance with orange throughout the living room, a village marketplace reminiscent of Africa or the Caribbean would line the kitchen cabinetry, while brown and stick flora would peek from behind a gold front door. On this door would hang a wreath woven with encouraging words waving to all who wandered by. TAKE THAT YOU TOP HGTV DESIGNERS!

I have grown into my style and not just in home décor, but in just me. Now I am determined to live in my style no matter what others think or the situation of the day. In fact, I have decided to surround me in my style, my muse, my passion, my spirit - me! Sure, I expect some: "What is that?", "Why would you do that?", "That's crazy!" Guess what? I get all of that and more anyway - why not get it for living in the style of ME?

Designers on the rise make a name for themselves by expressing creativity that is not out of the box but totally away from the box. They also gain recognition by developing a unique personality in their styling. Their individual creativity and style is what draws people to them. They really cannot and will not be consumed with those who do not like what they bring to the table (or the table they brought to the room) - because they understand it is not about their style.

They have come to understand that their style does not have to be your style; yet it can be the perfect flair for the one whose spirit calls for it.

My darling designer, here is what I challenge you to do - create your own style magazine. Give it a name - PIZAZZ, WOW, YEAH BABY, or NOIR - whatever is you. Now write the stories that define your style and how you will embrace it in every aspect of your life. You are the cover story. You are the flavor of the season. This style is about you and you are something to behold!

Here is what I challenge you to do - create your own style magazine. Give it a name - PIZAZZ, WOW, YEAH BABY, or NOIR - whatever is you. Now write the stories that define your style and how you will embrace it in every aspect of your life. You are the cover story:

Today write your future

The Inauguration of a Dreamer

Barack Hussein Obama, was elected the 44th President of the United States of America in November of 2008, and made history by becoming the first Black President of the same. The election of Obama fulfills the dreams and visions of two powerful men who lived in the midst of this country's horrific and embarrassing Civil Rights struggle - Robert Kennedy and Dr. Martin Luther King Jr. In an early 60's interview, Dr. King said he believed a Negro American could be president within 25 years; Kennedy said in a national address (also in the early 60's) that he believed this country could heal and progress to the point that we could elect a Black president within 40 years. Their statements reflect the dreams and hopes of two men who despite seeing people at their worst - believed in their best. They had dreams not just for themselves but for a nation of people.

Interestingly, all of this tickled my mind after hearing two inspirational messages on dreams delivered at church. The Biblical scripture unfolded the life of Joseph and how his dreams caused him to be hated - literally by his brothers. His dreams so intimidated and disturbed them that after - what I call - pulling death straws; they sold their own flesh into slavery. From there Joseph obtained prominence, was lied on by a manipulative woman, was jailed and finally rose to prominence again.

Dreams, especially those that awaken your power and prominence, are intimidating. Your dreams are great as long as they quickly produce a tangible and financial reward and do so consistently. For some, that is definitely the divine path they will be favored with. For others, like Joseph, there are some seasons of hardships that must be undertaken in order that your position is sure and your faith is even more certain. You know what Joseph taught me? (I, like him, learned this a bit late) He taught me to keep my dreams securely wrapped in quiet prayer until they are strong enough to be revealed.

I presented my dreams too soon to some who are not designed to dream at my level and when the money tree did not quickly shake its massive leaves to blanket the lawn on either side of the house; temporary applauders became strong oppositional forces. I know how Joseph must have felt and even though I know without a doubt God assigned a season of attacks to me and appointed me to whoop its behind. Even with that knowledge, the growing and testing of one's faith is still hard. I am a stronger person because of it and I am so proud of me; for I did not run and every time I was knocked to the ground- I got up. That I believe is the mark of a true dreamer - knowing that you have to fight for the dream and sometimes fight repeatedly.

In early 2009, my son and I were covered by a friend who quietly respects my dreams; she and a handful of others would often tell me that I have a calling to pull people's dreams out of them. I am not sure how true that is, but I am now convinced that is part of the deeper roots that sprout my dreams. Doing it - pulling out people's dreams, is also part of those deeper roots and I believe it is the part that pisses off the negative forces around me. If I dream, if I fight for my dream, if I reach inside you to pull a dream to the surface - I am creating too much positive energy, too much hope, too much light and too much of God's essence.

Well, okay dreamer, join me today in pissing off dream killers – let's inaugurate hope in our lives. Stand up, grab your Bible or your tool of inspiration and write your address to the world about who you are and what your dreams bring to the table. What does your inauguration address say about hope, fighting for your dreams, allowing your sincere, divine dream to pull you through hell? What does your inauguration address say about who you are destined to be? Does your inauguration address have the power of a dreamer and the audacity of hope? Dream on my child and when someone comes - and someone will - to challenge your dreams and even snatch it from your bosom - tell them - GET OFF MY PILLOW!

Let's inaugurate hope in our lives. Stand up, grab your Bible or your tool of inspiration and write your address to the world about who you are and what your dreams bring to the table. What does your inauguration address say about hope, fighting for your dreams, allowing your sincere, divine dream to pull you through hell?:

Today write your future

_____

_____

_____

_____

_____

_____

_____

_____

_____

_____

_____

_____

_____

_____

_____

_____

A Will for the Demons in your Life

I walked into the MICU room of an Atlanta-area hospital, the sound of what I viewed to be a massive respirator greeted me. There on the hospital bed was my uncle - my favorite uncle. Yet, the lifeless shell said something very obvious - he was no longer there. Yes, he had aged; he had grown thinner, though he was never a large man. He was gone. The task of removing him from life support still had to be made. As I stroked his hair on that Friday evening and rubbed his shoulder, I thought about how life really is available only for the precise second we inhale and exhale.

My uncle officially died on a Saturday morning. However, for a man who lived his life by his terms, not caring what anyone else thought - he died the moment that determination to be him left. It left, according to the doctor, with the initial stroke that landed him in MICU three to four days earlier. I thought about all of the little things that he had taught me over the years - through his spoken advice and his actions. While I did not always agree with what he did, he was always true to himself, even admitting that he could not overcome the narcotic demons that had plagued him since his military service in Vietnam. He lived his life, by his terms, yet tormented by demons. Demons - addictive, negative, defeating, disturbing, damning, damaging and tormenting behaviors, habits, practices and mindsets.

I can say the same thing. For there are some "demons" figuratively and perhaps even literally speaking that some of us have struggled with for years. If we put aside the spiritual arguments, jargon and rhetoric long enough, most of us can confess that the demons may be of a sexual nature, a financial nature, a health nature or even an emotional nature - yet we struggle with them and every once in awhile they get the best of us. Until we decide that enough is enough and we send the demons back to hell. I have often heard older women say to younger women involved in bad relationships, "Baby when you get good and tired, and you have had enough, then you'll do something about it." I believe the same holds true for our demons.

These boogers put a significant part of our lives on respirators. We have to get to the point when we decide to take the demons off of life support. Their living will has been the presence and participation in our lives in a haunting and often devastating manner. A dear friend and mentor, is also an attorney who specializes in estate planning. I have marveled at the details of some of the cases she has studied and have witnessed firsthand how accurate she is in proclaiming every one should have documents in place detailing their desires in the event of incapacity and death. I realized as we watched my uncle's body react to the welcoming seconds of death, that I did not want to go a step further in my life with the pressure of negative behaviors and practices weighing me down.

I have decided to write them out of my will. So why don't you do the same? This will is a bit different, because in it, you are going to list each and every demon. Instead of listing what you are leaving them upon your demise; you are listing what you are taking back from them and restoring in a powerful and meaningful way in your life.

To the demon of making financial decisions from a place of desperation, I take back every dollar lost in the process by creating and diligently following a sound budget and financial plan.

To the demon of obesity, I take back good health by making wiser eating choices and by following an exercise plan that is effective and comfortable for me.

You get the picture. How wild is that, writing a last will and testament for the demons that subconsciously become intrinsic parts of our nature? To those demons, leave a first class ticket back to hell.

I have decided to write them out of my will. This will is a bit different, because in it, you are going to list each and every demon. Instead of listing what you are leaving them upon your demise; you are listing what you are taking back from them and restoring in a powerful and meaningful way in your life:

Today write your future

Why is there a Coffin Under There

As darkness slid into her comfortable home making way for the sun to stand guard, an intriguing vision grabbed my attention. This vision revealed a lovely room, reminiscent of large and breezy plantation homes. White sheets covered everything. I was speaking to two ladies in the room when I stumbled across something covered by a crisp sheet tucked in at its corners. One of the women turned to face me as I inquired about what I had stumbled on. I moved the sheet away and to my surprise there was a beautiful caramel colored wood coffin.

It shocked me but did not scare me. The woman explained, very matter-of-factly, that she just had not been ready to bury it. I never asked her who or what was in it, nor did the other woman. I did ask why she was not ready to bury it. She simply shrugged her shoulders and responded, "Just not ready." My conscious self took over and I smiled because I realized I had just been blessed to have one of my dream reality sessions with God. (By the way, these are absolutely much better than ANY reality TV show.) I wondered how many of us keep coffins buried beneath sheets or situations or busy work because we just are not ready to bury them. I wondered what we keep in our coffins.

This woman held on to, and clearly moved from place to place, a coffin; a home for dead things, because she was not ready to allow the death of relationships, consequences, bad decisions, unfortunate moves and other truths of life to have their final moment. Therefore, she held on to the coffin, carefully covering it and taking care to assure it was tucked in. Sadly, I have to admit that I have held onto some coffins or perhaps one big coffin full of dead things that I have refused to bury or have feared burying. Is it possible that we hold on to the coffin because we want to be able to mourn when it is convenient, grieve when it is easier than pressing on or be consoled when we really need to be challenged? The coffin allows us to feel sorry for ourselves.

Funerals are without doubt one of the most traumatic and heart-wrenching life events; yet they are also an opportunity to celebrate life, experiences and reflect on legacy. Yet when we hold on to the coffin, we fail to release the life that was moving into its next assignment. What would happen if you (and if I) finally buried our fear, our reservations, our numerous and unfounded concerns about the what-ifs, and our ability to convince ourselves that we cannot _____
(you fill in the blanks). What would happen if you (and I) stopped hiding our coffins and using them as a prayer altar? What would happen if we finally decided to bury the dead things as opposed to allowing them to accompany us in the dance of life?

I want to encourage you to take a deep breath and write out the burial plans for the coffin in your life. Write out its obituary and script out what the coffin takes with it – understanding that only the lesson from it can remain. Think about this - clearly, if there is a coffin, death was imminent and necessary. What can holding on to dead things produce in your current moment? May these words serve as a shovel for us as we begin to dig the grave where our coffins will finally rest? Now plan your repast and celebrate the life that death has brought to your door.

What would happen if we finally decided to bury the dead things as opposed to allowing them to accompany us in the dance of life? I want to encourage you to take a deep breath and write out the burial plans for the coffin in your life. Write out its obituary and script out what the coffin takes with it:

Today write your future

_____

_____

_____

_____

_____

_____

_____

_____

_____

_____

_____

_____

_____

_____

_____

_____

I Could have been more Disobedient but I am So Glad God Kicked me into Obedience Instead

I was blessed to reconnect with a wonderful group of loving, caring and compassionate women as part of a Bible study group. I did not share anything - instead I listened. I returned to this fold somewhat of a prodigal child. After a friend/business associate/fellow believer said to me over my Shaken Iced Tea Lemonade (black tea sweetened, thank you very much) that God led her to tell me that I have been disobedient. Had I have been the woman I was years ago, I probably would have slapped the words from her mouth and cut her verbally. I did neither. Primarily because I had been asking God for months what was going on with me. I was feeling disconnected, every financial vessel either had dried up or was behaving really wacky, and the strangest things kept popping up in every area of my life. Thus, if you ask, He will answer - especially when He knows you are in a place to finally listen. Secondly, she did not come to me rambling, but she came with Biblical passages that spoke directly to me and said, in essence, this is your final warning, chick! We agreed that I would turn off everything later that evening and I would pray about my disobedience and she would support me in prayer.

What I learned is that I have the uncanny ability to use the very things God instilled in me against God. Imagine that! I use my stubbornness, my ability to assess and then respond with what I think is best, and my ability to analyze the color orange off of an orange against God. I do it so well that I had not realized there were some areas where I was being God (in the wrong sense) in my life. I do it so well that I had not realized that I questioned my worth to do the most important thing that He called me to do - minister - not realizing that questioning my worthiness meant questioning Him and His ability to call me to do something great.

One of the things I ask God repeatedly (from the moment I first heard Him say teach my daughters) is, "What do I have to say to anybody about anything?" "Why does what I have to say matter?" Well in that study group, He responded. It was not only my first night back in forever, but another young lady returned as well. When I came in, she was sharing how wonderfully God had been turning some things around in her life. In the midst of sharing, she looked at me and shared that often in her struggles, she thought about my hard situations I'd shared with the group; and knowing that I kept moving in spite of them helped her. Later in the discussion, she recalled how I sent an email to this praying group of women, comparing my trials and my trust to Job; it was the focal passage on the handout being discussed in that setting. She said that email encouraged her. She actually encouraged me, Without even knowing it, God sent her on assignment to show me a powerful purpose that I possess. Because I moved in obedience that night - I was in place so that she could plant what she was supposed to.

I almost missed that moment, because in my disobedience, I joined another church and immediately my spirit yelled GET OUT! After attending only one Sunday service and two Bible studies, I had to beg the pastor's forgiveness and obediently go back to where God had placed me. My assignment there was not finished. In fact I had run from it. You see on my way to a Sunday service about a year or so prior to reconnecting with the group, I clearly heard God say that I was to minister by leading a women's study group at the church I was attending. After service that day, the bubbly leader of our group informed me that she had (or was) going to talk to the campus pastor about my leading a group. I was thrown off but not surprised. Months later when I felt that nudge again - I took off like an Olympic sprinter - telling God and anyone who would listen that I was disconnected and I needed more. The more I needed was in giving what God has taught me. The disconnection was because I wasn't doing the more.

Hear this - God will not shut up and we can stick our fingers in our ears until we are 158 years old, He will be heard. In my valley of disobedience God sent a Yoruba priestess, a New Age reverend, a minister who has never laid eyes on me (and has called me Min. Freeman from the moment she told me to walk in my calling), a spiritual numerologist and a former and prospective client to tell me the same thing - you are called into a higher level of ministry, you have a spiritual calling all over you, you were born with a gift of teaching and counseling. It is not about ordination - it is about helping, serving and teaching truth. They all said the exact same things and then God sent a fellow Christian to open my eyes to this truth - the more that I needed was in giving what God has taught me and I had been disobedient to His voice for too long. I rejoice because while God sent the locusts to eat up what He had blessed me with, His Word also assures me that He will restore what was lost if I sincerely repent, fast, pray and stop being so unbelievably hard-headed with Him.

Disobedience blocks us! There is no need to sugar coat it or make it sound nice. Your disobedient behavior and intellectual rationalizations are why things are not flowing exceedingly, abundantly above what you can think or ask. I have come into the light. I have applied the salve of renewed trust on my wounds of chastisement, and I am moving in obedience. Baby, I have been in the storm too long. Disobedience blocks us! Here is your writing assignment; the scripture in Joel (2:25) indicates that God sent four types of locusts to devour the provisions of the people: swarming, crawling, consuming and chewing. Trust me when I considered this passage thoroughly I could clearly see some swarming, crawling, consuming and chewing happening. Can you? Write the areas in your life where locusts were sent to devour potentially because of your disobedience. Now write an action plan to correct - immediately - those disobedient thoughts, spirits and actions. Confess your disobedience and sincerely apologize and turn away from it. Then you can stand with me as we wait for restoration. I will let you in on a little secret; it has already started for me! Go get yours!

Here is your writing assignment; Write the areas in your life where locusts were sent to devour potentially because of your disobedience. Now write an action plan to correct - immediately - those disobedient thoughts, spirits and actions:

Today write your future

_____

_____

_____

_____

_____

_____

_____

_____

_____

_____

_____

_____

_____

_____

The Oil - Overfilled

I want to share a very profound and deeply spiritual moment for me. Surely, by now you have figured out that I am in love with and loved by God. Nothing in me is separate from Him. What I want to share hopefully will challenge you as it has done for me.

In the spring of 2010, my little Mitsubishi (which was already falling apart and would become a river whenever it rained) was totaled in an accident. Three weeks later, God had a friend give me $1000 to buy another set of wheels or put a down payment on a vehicle. I opted to find something used but reliable because I needed to be positioned to grow my business, and a car payment was not in that equation. I found a car for $700 and I was on the road again! YAY! Four days into owning the car, there was a problem. I discovered, haphazardly, that the oil gauge did not work. This discovery was made only after I poured way too much oil into the car, trying to make that oil gauge rise. I was slightly bummed out about it, yet did not believe that it was anything major.

On the night I realized there was a problem, I'd dropped one niece off at the movies and the other younger niece and I headed home. We did not make it. So much smoke was coming from the rear and hood of the car; we pulled into a parking lot and called for someone to come get us. I was distressed. It was dark and she and I were sitting in a parking lot. She asked what was wrong with the car and I explained it. I also told her that God did not bless me with the car to take it away with a silly mechanical problem. She understood it as best she could for a five year old. Then, in that moment, God had her share with me the Easter story that she'd learned in children's church and she ended with, "Auntie we have to remember to tell God thank you every day." So, we told God thank you at that moment for the car, for the smoke and for the person coming to get us.

Shortly after that, during the wee hours of the morning I woke up and after allowing my mind to run through every personal and business matter, I finally said, "Ok God, clearly you want to talk to me, so I am listening."

He asked, "Is your gauge working?"

My mind immediately went to the car - "No, it isn't."

He inquired again, "Is your gauge working? Do you know that your oil is overflowing?"

I knew at that moment, He was not talking about the car, but He was talking about me. In Biblical terms, the oil represents anointing, the thing in which you are spiritually called out or ordained to do/be/abide in. God very clearly said to me in that conversation, that I keep reading my oil gauge as empty or too low, when in fact it is overflowing. My gauge, my mindsets, my confidence - kept registering low oil - it was a false reading.

Clearly, at that point in the conversation, I was blown away; yet He wasn't finished. Here is what I learned. The mechanic said to me that when you put too much oil in a car, it has to come out. A car will find a way to get rid of it: it burns it off, it forces it to leak out, it pushes it through filters and at some point before the damage happens, you have to change the oil and clean up the leaks and spills. What I learned as God brought this all back to me; is that there is so much anointing (oil) in me that it is looking for a way to get out. It is burning off the things that keep my gauge broken and my perception and acceptance of my anointing being low. It is pushing to come out because it is too abundant to sit in my life (engine) and it wants to operate.

Finally, the mechanic kept saying to me, and I kept hearing his words as God spoke to me, "its okay, the car is fine, it is not damaged, and it's a good car." I kept hearing his words in the midst of God's words, because I needed to know that although my gauge was broken; my vision/my dream is still intact and the oil is still flowing and active. Is your gauge broken? Does your hopes, dreams, and calling gauge always read empty or low? Now ask yourself, the question I asked myself - WHY?

Today's writing assignment is to draw a gauge that is indicative of your life and mark the point on that gauge that represents where your calling is. Then write your mechanics notes to repair the damage and get to the place of your calling. My gauge was broken, but wonderfully there is another way to test the measure of oil in your life and that is to seek God and hear Him when He speaks. Is your gauge broken?

I needed to know that although my gauge was broken; my vision/my dream is still intact and the oil is still flowing and active. Is your gauge broken? Draw a gauge that is indicative of your life and mark the point on that gauge that represents where your calling is. Then write your mechanics notes to repair the damage and get to the place of your calling:

Today write your future

Talk to the Hand

Can you believe she said that? (Whatever **that** was) Moreover, she said it with some sense of power in your life! Can you believe he had the intestinal fortitude to say something that off-handed about you? (Whatever that **something** was) Even more bewildering, he had the audacity to say it with some sense of power in your life! Well, how about that!

I'm often around people who feel it necessary and absolutely okay to say whatever they choose about my decisions and my capacity of being. That would be okay if I asked for their opinions – which are usually negative, based on their world or far away from my divine conversations. I have learned to engage in a disengaged conversation with them until they are done preaching their correction to me. It has also been my experience that opinions cannot be solicited from everyone. You see, some believe that once their opinion is voiced, it is in fact a directive that you should act on immediately. Troubling is the reality that for many of us we do take the opinions of others as mandates for our lives.

For a long time, I would obsess on the things those people said or thought about me, my personal vision, my personal dreams, my no sense of fashion, the fact that I like to keep my finger and toe nails long - even my hair style. Then I started writing the left of what they thought was right. In other words I would write the truth - my truth - and that overruled their opinion. I honestly believe that anyone who gets caught up in the exterior of anything never fully sees its beauty nor experiences its spectacular abilities. So, those who offer sought and un-sought opinions may say it is right and perhaps it is - for them, or even for you. However, the decision as to its proper place in your world must be yours completely. A decision to live someone else's personal responses also means you make a decision to live someone else's consequences.

Remember in pre-school or kindergarten, when you would take your favorite colored-crayon and trace your hand - wasn't that the coolest? Take a look at your hand now, trace your left hand and pen what is left in your life after you silence all of the other people's opinions, beliefs, notions and attitudes. If everything is silenced, you have QUIET. In the quiet, you should begin to HEAR - your true spirit, which means you will sense DIVINE DIRECTION. Imagine that you have never heard any opinion or thought about what you should do; and instead with each lifeline you draw on that left hand, list a purpose for your life, list an item or person that brings a smile or sense of joy, list something silly that makes you laugh. On your lifelines dream again - what would you be if you could be anything in the world and how would you become it? Strange, now look at what you created without everyone's input? A dream and a plan to go get it.

It is something about that left hand. What is left? Left is to edify you, left is to remind you that it is your thought patterns and God's thought streams that matter, left is to direct you to divine power – for you can do all things... you are more than a conqueror, and why would you expect anyone to understand a "peculiar people?" Peculiar are those who would put extreme faith in the unseen and bring its truth to dynamic realities. What is left? Left is your power, in your hand, to be used for your edification. Talk to the hand and it will certainly tell you some awesome things about YOU!

Remember in pre-school or kindergarten, when you would take your favorite colored-crayon and trace your hand - wasn't that the coolest? Take a look at your hand now, trace your left hand and pen what is left in your life after you silence all of the other people's opinions, beliefs, notions and attitudes. With each lifeline you draw on that left hand, list a purpose for your life, list an item or person that brings a smile or sense of joy, list something silly that makes you laugh.

Today write your future

Turning on my Power

There are just certain songs that make us realize or celebrate different parts of our power and our significance. Those songs may change from time to time; while some will always have a lasting impact. I used to work with a guy that would laugh at me, because he discovered if he wanted to knock me off balance for a few moments all he needed to do was play LOVE BALLAD by LTD. The song still awakens the power of passionate love in me. A few years ago I discovered a track on an Anthony Hamilton CD, I think the title is PASS ME OVER, but the spirit of that song spoke to me - if I am dreaming don't wake me, don't disturb that special spiritual conversation for me. The song speaks to the wonderful power to dream in me. Finally, there is never a time I listen to Lamar Campbell's CLOSER that I am going to listen to it only once or listen without coming to tears. The song speaks to the power of loving God close enough to realize when you mess up nothing will be right until you get close to Him again. For some, your seasonal power songs may be the slamming Mary J. Blige, FINE, or Kerri Hilson's PRETTY GIRL ROCK. It might be Yolanda Adams's BE BLESSED, or Martha Munizzi's rendition of BECAUSE OF WHO YOU ARE. Or Jonathan Butler's FALLING IN LOVE WITH JESUS. These songs ignite a certain power within.

For a span of about a year, I struggled with feeling as if my life was not connecting. God and I are closer now then we have ever been, and through understanding and examining Him through other faiths, I have developed a deeper intimacy as a Christian. God recently showed me something about myself and I had to laugh realizing that He (of course) was absolutely correct about the character flaw He shined His spotlight on. Then as I read the third Chapter of the Biblical book of

Ephesians, I was hit right in the middle of my big old pecan tan forehead, (just beneath the spot where the gray is growing in and just above the spot where my naturally arched eyebrows grow) about that character flaw and my feeling of disconnect.

I got the disconnection within when God pulled something out of my memory bank. When we were kids growing up on NW 52 Street, and then NW 177 Terrace in South Florida, there were times we would experience black outs - especially in the summer. Yet, we would not hide indoors; instead parents would take to their front porches and kids would play in the dark as though the streets lights were still illuminating our surroundings. We knew that while power wasn't channeling light to our street, there still was undoubtedly power that would be re-ignited. We never questioned that there was power somewhere and it would show up again.

Ephesians 3: 7 reads: of which I became a minister according to the gift of the grace of God given to me by the effective working of His power.

Ephesians 3:16-17 reads: that He would grant you, according to the riches of His glory to be strengthened (empowered) with might through His Spirit in the inner man. That Christ may dwell in your hearts through faith.

Finally, **Ephesians 3: 20-21 records:** Now to Him who is able to do exceedingly, abundantly above all that we ask or think, according to the power that works in us.

Now, I'm a reader and when I read, there are just lines (if written well) that will jump off the page and speak to my intellect, my creativity and my understanding. That happened as I read these three areas of verse. The things that jumped out at me all have to do with understanding that there is already a divine power within and God will do amazing things for you and through you when you work with what is already in you. Seriously? Seriously. The lines that jumped for me:

From verse 7 - the effective working of His power.

From verse 16 - to be strengthened with might through His Spirit in the inner man.

And, while I have done the benediction in church for years, I missed the POWER of the word ACCORDING in verse 21 until it popped me in the forehead. It says He is able to do exceedingly, abundantly above all that we ask or think ACCORDING to the POWER THAT WORKS IN US.

I realized that like reactors somehow disconnect and power is lost to homes. I had somehow disconnected from the very power that God placed in me even before my birth. In this disconnect, I was trying to focus and see in the dark instead of focusing on the truth that there is power in me to bring light. My struggle had not been because I believed God could not handle my woes. My struggle came because I disconnected from the power He has already instilled. With my inner power disconnected, I move in only a shadow of what I am to be. When I do not effectively work His power within, then He can only do what my faith and my power gives Him room to do.

Oh, if you could have seen the look on my face as that revelation rested upon me! Today, I dare you to create your own power bill. How many kilowatts of faith are you working with? Where is the darkness awaiting your light? Have your reactors misfired or disconnected? Dude! Baby girl! - reach in and turn on your power, then work in it effectively, so that God can do exceedingly and abundantly above all that you can ask or think according to that power. I am so encouraged and I pray that my power connection is recharged, restored and re-energized because exceeding abundance and I have some things to do. What about you?

He is able to do exceedingly, abundantly above all that we ask or think ACCORDING to the POWER THAT WORKS IN US. I realized that like reactors somehow disconnect and power is lost to homes. I had somehow disconnected from the very power that God placed in me even before my birth. Today, I dare you to create your own power bill. How many kilowatts of faith are you working with? Where is the darkness awaiting your light?:

Today write your future

_____

_____

_____

_____

_____

_____

_____

_____

_____

_____

_____

_____

_____

_____

_____

The Couch's Bedtime Tale

My son goes through these very interesting moments when it comes to his sleeping habits. For no apparent reason, out of the blue, he will leave his place of slumber and sleep just feet away from my bed for a number of consecutive days. Then he just goes back to sleeping in his room. Poof! He also tends to get very upset with me, when I open the windows and then do not take the extra time to assure I lock them after I return them to their closed position. The manly security detail aside, it is the sleeping thing that baffles me.

When he was younger, he would do the same thing but he would climb into bed with me instead. Why does he do this? He has told me he doesn't know - he just does. Can I confess something? I love when he does it! Somehow, I feel that all is right and all is okay when I can hear that healthy (loud is a better word) snore rumbling from nearby.

There are times when the hustle and bustle of the day gets to be hectic, hellish and just plain old foolish. On those days, I often crawl into bed, a few feet from the heavenly throne and lay at God's feet. There I am comforted and I feel like all is right and all is well with my soul - even if I leave a bucket of tears there or just cry out incoherently. I wonder if his sleeping on the couch is my little man's way of telling me that he senses something in me and so he sleeps near in an effort to assure me that all is okay with him and thus all is really okay with me.

At the foot of the throne, I fall asleep quickly and soundly, much the way Mr. Man falls asleep quickly and soundly on the chair or floor near my bed. There is something about falling into slumber near our parent, near God, that makes rest a welcome activity. When you rest at the throne, there is amazing warmth that engulfs when God picks us up and places us safely in His arms. Then as if He is telling a gentle bedtime story, He talks to us in our dreams about those things that have felt hectic, hellish and just plain old foolish. He gives us a remedy for the moment or comfort when we simply need to face what is happening around us.

For many of us when we were children, our parents, or perhaps a sibling or a babysitter would read us a bedtime story. Aah to be a kid again – and you can! Take some time to write a fairy tale just for you. Pen a fairy tale that features God, as the Ultimate Hero, coming to save the day, and you as the fair prince or princess who has been granted a seat next to His throne. What will your fairy tale reveal? (Don't forget to draw colorful pictures, use a big 64-piece crayon box).

When is the last time you fell asleep at the foot of the throne? When is the last time you heard the wonderful bedtime story that only The Divine can tell you - no fairy tale, no forced happy ending - but His wonderful truth, promises and assurances to be there? What a wonderful place to find rest, where The Father can gather you into the blanket of His wings.

Goodnight my sweet one.

For many of us when we were children, our parents, or perhaps a sibling or a babysitter would read us a bedtime story. Aah to be a kid again – and you can! Take some time to write a fairy tale just for you. Pen a fairy tale that features God, as the Ultimate Hero, coming to save the day:

Today write your future

Why Now?

I am a very active dreamer. In one of those pretty non-descript life seasons, I had the most wonderful and yet bothersome dream. I have always been single. Sure, I have been involved, but marriage was never on the table. Like a lot of sisters, I went through those periods of loneliness, extreme loneliness and *OH GOD WHY HAST THOU FORSAKEN ME* when it came to jumping the broom and thus experienced men and relationships that were not for me.

Then, with a new Godly-encounter, I began to like me and do those things that I and me like doing together. I also became a mom and began to do all those wonderful little things that new moms do (okay so initially I failed in the remembering to feed the child department, but I got the hang of it). The two things combined, did what being a workaholic never cured - turned the loneliness into a wonderful kind of love. When I got to that comfort with self and loving my son, I never thought about marriage constantly anymore nor do I have those *OH GOD WHY HAST THOU FORSAKEN ME* moments anymore. Did God and I talk about what I wanted and needed to experience in a relationship? Absolutely. Did I spell out what I was willing to accept for me and define what was really going to impress me beyond the superficial? Yes! I was clear and very detailed in every area and so I moved forward. I was content and am content in being single knowing this is the season for it in my life.

Oh, the dream! I have to set it up first by explaining that I have a major schoolgirl kind of crush on Actor Dennis Haysbert, the lead guy from the television show The Unit and the Allstate commercial guy. Have mercy! In any event, in this dream, some friends, my little niece and I were at some kind of flea market thing and there was this guy there, with a voice like Haysbert's and about as tall, with nice hands. Why I paid attention to them – I have no clue. He introduced himself and immediately became very comfortable in the way he spoke to me; and in what seemed like an instant was endeared to me. In this dream, my friends, niece and I hung out for awhile, and he hung out with us. He and I went back and forth gleaning information from each other through a long list of questions and challenging responses. What caught me off guard in this dream is that in the course of walking and talking, in a very natural, non-thought kind of matter, he put his arm around me and I was warmly in place. That moment was so amazingly real for me, that I woke up feeling his arm around me, and asking God, "Why now?"

It occurred to me as I thought about a very loving relationship a dear friend of mine is involved in and an absolutely-not relationship another dear friend was potentially entering that perhaps the dream came to tell me there is something I needed to be reminded of. That is, there are still remnants of the woman that loves hard, sincerely and passionately within me and her season may be drawing near. The why now has a lot to do with several things: health challenges, growing a business that is still in its finding balance stages, a son hitting puberty hard and preparing to go to middle school and on and on and on...

The why now comes from a place of knowing that the romantic in me - if I allow her to, will always supersede the woman that knows the Bible says to guard your heart. When the romantic shows up, I got you flowers, sounds like; *he's gonna love me forever!* I showered after awakening from the dream and felt my skin come alive as I used a former client's bath product - Yeyefini's Mango Ginger Sugar Scrub; a scrub she makes at home that is absolutely decadent. I laughed remembering her instructions to use it and go out in public so "that man" would find me. Why now - is never about our timing is it? It is about the fact that if we took the time to do everything we believe we need to do in order to do what we believe we want/must/need or are called to do - we won't do a thing. This is not the time to be in love or put marriage back on the list of prayers for me - at least that's what I say. Yet somehow, I believe divinity is saying otherwise and so a sister is guarding her heart and looking for that warm hug so hot it wakes you from slumber. If he does not come for another five or ten years - it's all good. For even in love, romance and passion, I have learned what it is to abound and be abased.

We have already written a love letter to ourselves on this journey; let's write a love letter for the lover that comes to us in our dreams. She or he may be in your life already, or the intensity of the love they can potentially bring may only exist in your dream. It does not matter. What matters is that you can define the love you desire and the love you can give and express it through your words. When you do, why now can be answered, because - I have loved you into being.

Let's write a love letter for the lover that comes to us in our dreams. You can define the love you desire and the love you can give and express it through your words:

Today write your future

About the Author

E. Claudette Freeman spent some 24 years in radio in South Florida, before leaving to obtain her Certified Life Coaching Credentials through the American Association of Christian Therapists and to start her own media corporation, Emily C. Freeman Holdings, LLC. The company does business through **E. Claudette Freeman Literary Services** which provides an array of writing services including: coaching, editing, commissioned stage/film works and publishing consulting. Employing literary principles and styling to empowerment modules, Freeman also hosts The Arise Center for Literary Healing, in home/conference and workplace based life coaching programs.

The company also delves into the publishing arena through **Pecan Tree Publishing.** PTP works with authors in various genres who have decided to self-publish, marrying traditional and print-on-demand amenities. PTP also publishes anthologies focusing on a variety of subject matters and produces four digital Christian-themed publications: PARABLES, SPIRIT RISING, OIKONOMIA and BELOVED.

As a writer, Freeman's honors include placing for two consecutive years in the Quest Theatre of West Palm Beach Loften Mitchell New Playwrights' Festival, being a featured reader in the Miami Book Fair International's WRITE IN OUR MIDST PROGRAM, being chosen as an apprentice to famed African-American author Ntozake Shange, during the Atlantic Center For The Arts Masters Residency Program, co-authoring the touring production of CHARCOAL SKETCHES, a play based on the lives of Zora Neale Hurston, Augusta Savage and Mary McLeod Bethune and being commissioned to author a Black history production FROM THE PORCH starring Danny Glover by the Miami Sports and Exhibition Authority.

She is the author of the collection of short stories: **PIECES AND THE STUFF THAT WAKES ME UP AT NIGHT;** a novel **SHELTERED DELIVERANCE,** three invigorating and engaging journals **THE MORNING HOUR: ARISE, WRITE, RELEASE; FABULOUS YOU: POWER NUGGETS FOR THE MOMENT** and **IF I WRITE IT, IT CAN HEAL**. She is also the author/producer of three literary CDs: **DRAMA EXPOSED** (fiction and poetry) **FOR THE BROTHA YOU ARE** (poetry) and SPIRIT AWAKENING (poetry); as well as several plays. She is currently working on two novels: one with former NBA Player Rory Sparrow, **YOU HAVE TO FILL THE NEED,** and a second about a woman's supernatural journey to awakening called **WHEN I DANCED WITH GOD.** She serves as a literary coach and editor to writers in various genres. Freeman lives in South Florida with her son Isaiah Langston-Michael Freeman, and their dog Missy.

www.ingramcontent.com/pod-product-compliance
Lightning Source LLC
Chambersburg PA
CBHW071708040426
42446CB00011B/1975